things change,

sometimes I stay the same

things change, sometimes I stay the same
by Alina Vitto
Paperback Edition

Reading Community Partners

First Published in 2023 by

Inkfeathers Publishing
Vivek Vihar, New Delhi 110095
www.inkfeathers.com

ISBN 978-81-19483-03-7

things change,

sometimes I stay the same

Alina Vitto

INKFEATHERS PUBLISHING
www.inkfeathers.com

READING COMMUNITY PARTNERS

Frob
Friends of books

Contents

the middle

To the reader.

Enjoy the journey.

"I don't know where to put my love,

Do I wait for time to do what it does?"

– Florence and the Machine, My Love, Dance Fever (2022)

(my words are yours now)

Dear reader,
Breathe.
I ask you to
Let go.

I ask you to
Escape,
Your solemn reality.

Allow me to,
Shelter you.

As you breathe in
My words,
I ask you to let go
Of your tears,
Let them find a home,
Staining the pages of this book.

Let your joy reach me;
Let me feel your pain.

Shed your burdens.
Allow me to provide you
With what you need;
Of what you're deprived.

Be it
The comfort of your bed,
Or the warmth of a mother never had.

If you require reassurance,
Or if you desire protection,
Allow me to hold your heart
If it is too heavy.

Let my words provide a retreat.
Let me heal your wounds.

I plant my lips,

To your forehead

And I hand you my daisies,

And in return,

I ask you to be gentle,

To the pieces of my soul,

That I now share with you.

Exhale, beloved,

For your pain too, shall pass,

And even in the dead of the night,

The sun too, shall rise.

Introduction

Alina Vitto

(Sudden, never fleeting)

The word I'd use
To describe us,
Would be, 'sudden'.

Sudden—but not fleeting,
Like the way I'd look at you,
Or our fits of laughter, and
Maybe, like the plans we'd made.

Yeah, sudden—but not fleeting,
Like it was at the beginning.

When you'd leave kisses
On my hands,
And call me when you were away.

And sudden, but not fleeting,
The smell of jasmine,
That used to plague my dreams.

And sudden, but not fleeting,
Right in the middle,
Maybe in my chest,
Or maybe in the palm of your hand.

And sudden,
But not fleeting.

Just like it was in the end.

The beginning

(Of spring.)

I watch from my bench,

The winter turn to wind,

The cold to colour,

My turmoil and tears, to dew drops.

I wear yellow,

The first taste of spring.

It seems as though she approved,

Of my choices, dressing in yellow herself.

I look out to the park,

The colours litter the centre.

As if she had heard us speak.

It was like an announcement.

"I am awake now.
I know you have been awaiting me."

Her voice is gentle, but
loud.

I feel the light that day.
I find the strength to cry, the next.

I find my joy now.

I get a lick of spring.

And yes,
I cannot wait to watch the flowers bloom.

And along with it,
My lover's face.

(Euphoria)

It was euphoria,

The way she touched me.

The way she spoke was magic.

The way her hands found mine.

I was bewitched.

Bewitched by the way she moved

By the butterflies I felt around her.

It was beautiful.

And it was safe.

I was safe.

She was my protector.

A safety net to catch my fallen heart.

It was home.

It was wrong too.

But it was her,

And it was euphoria.

(Remains)

A part of my heart
Lies in my chest, thundering at the sight of you.
Pouring out love like water,
Breaking like glass
The shards piercing my skin.

Another
disappeared a long time ago.
Sailed the depths of the sea,
Watched the earth spin,
And got lost with the wind.

The beloved traveller still writes me letters.

One,
Stays in a book, maybe

Or perhaps under the sun in dehra,

resting,

Till we meet again.

A smaller replica

Hangs from a silver chain.

Another

Blossoms in my garden.

Some of it

Is etched onto flimsy white papers,

Locked away, sealed in yellow-stained envelopes

Too pure for any other to taint.

But

Rest assured,

My love, for forever

A part of my heart,

Sits on the heel of your right palm,

Carefully drawn

In blue ink.

And if you asked,

I'd pluck out every flower,

Give up the chain,

Steal the sun,

Rip out the pages to every book,

Sail the darkest sea,

And split open my chest.

just so you know

That I love you most ardently.

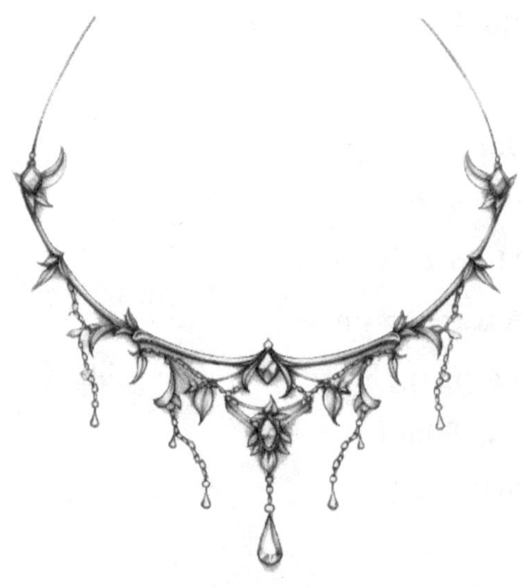

(Sleep)

Come back, my love

Quit your worrying,

And come back to me.

Though I don't pretend to understand,

All that flows through,

And washes ashore the banks of your mind,

Knotted tighter than the roots of my flowers.

I ask you not,

To now wonder,

What lies beyond the pond

Which your wondering soul has created.

Oh, and what of the hypocrite

I must be,

For I pretend like I too, do not wonder,

As much as you.

Alas,

It is hard to limit or contain,

The mind, in its travels

Much to my dismay.

But

Fall asleep, dearest,

For tomorrow's world awaits you.

Sleep, beloved,

For we can ponder at dawn.

(It is far too late for my worries)

I lay awake,
Watching the wake
Of the sleepless night,
And my soul aches.

I soon celebrate
The years of my life and
So much if it I waste,
Longing to see your face.

oh, but dearest,
I do not complain,
For I'd spend lifetimes
In vain
Only for your gaze.

I'd cross oceans to see you,

And an ocean is what it feels like,

Sitting on my balcony.

When in reality,

It's only but a walk,

Then tell me why

It seems as though the whole sea

Has set its heart on you not seeing me.

(False hope)

Oh, darling,

I ask you to be kind

To your lover,

To keep in mind

That it is the heart of your lover,

That you have managed to chain.

It pains

To be unsure

If you still feel the same.

Or if all the games

Ain't what I think.

Allow me just a moment,

To be weak,

Am I wrong to seek,

Your actions or your words?

Is it wrong of me to freak,

If it feels like your love retreats,

Every time I hear her shriek?

Won't you grant your lover reassurance?

Give me some kind of promise?

I am aware of your lack of faith,

In forevers,

And I am aware of the impossibility of

This endeavour.

But I ask you to entertain me,

And try, for the sake of my sanity.

(Warning: proceed with caution)

I've dreamt of love
From storybooks.
I've written pages,
Made it sound like a plant,
Growing and growing,
Blooming like flowers,
Blazing like the sun.
I've spun words like webs
Of yearning and wanting
And having.
I've spoken of gentle touches
And lingering glances.

But

Somewhere along the line,

I've failed to mention the pain,

The wilting,

The sun's setting,

The tears,

The unheard sobs, the screams.

I've not warned the lover of

The quiet rocking,

Back and forth,

In the dimmed yellow lights.

Wondering,

'Why.

Why, if you loved me so,

Would you not tell me?'

Why would you not touch me,

Why would you just smile,

Why would you stay so far away?

Am I too much?

Or

Am I not enough?

Why—even through a lens —

Can't you see,

That

There is not a future that exists

For me,

Without the thought of you.

Not a version of me,

Without your shadow.

Not a body of mine,

Without your handprints.

And

I don't ask much of you.

All I ask is

For you to let me be enough.

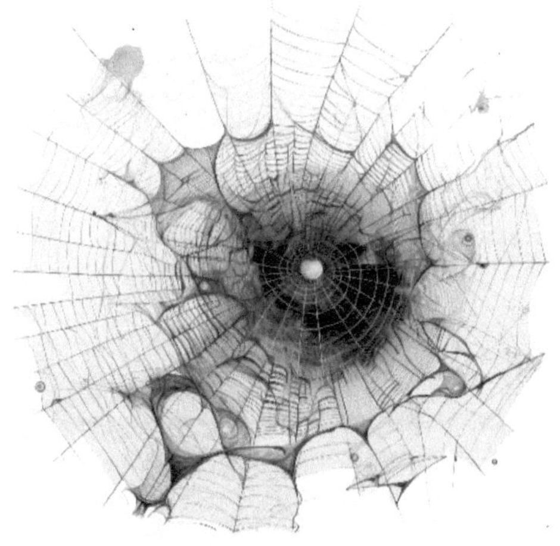

(Maybe, the planning hurts the both of us)

I had plans, you know,
Of a house behind a creek,
A crooked brown fence,
Children,
Not our own,
Who stop by for flowers,
The ones from my garden.

A warm full house
That reminded you of my own.

Or even a small room,
With just the two of us,
Existing.
that would work too.

But,
Our warmth filled kitchen,
Started getting cold,

The creek dried up,

All my 'we's and 'our's became

'me's and 'your's

March 27—as I laid that flower,

To rest in the mud,

I left with it,

My dreams,

Our home,

Your love.

and I knew even then

That nothing would ever be the same.

(Maybe: i)

Maybe we were meant to be,
Just not in the way we thought.

Maybe,
Our souls were
Ripped apart from the same star,
But our hearts, never meant to touch.

Maybe it was written on some stone.
I was to give you
My all, and expect nothing back,
No damages for my fall.

Maybe it was only me,
Who was to fall in love,
And you to remain
Indifferent.
In your thoughts,
I was to never cross.

Maybe it was just me

Who deserved your worst,

Watch the others take your highs,

As I stood in the corner with your lows,

Because,

Maybe, you were the burning fire,

And I was simply meant to be your coal.

(and maybe it was never fine,

I was just blind to it all.)

The middle

(I want to rip my heart straight down the middle.)

I've learnt to hate silver,
And never more
Have I wished
To burn it.

I've learnt the power my words hold,
Never once
Was I ever taught,
To control them.

I've been forced to feel
Every emotion,
I've put to paper,
And I still haven't learnt how to not let it
Destroy me.

(Guest of wind)

I had a visitor in the wind,
Today.

She rattled at my door,
And all my plants swayed,
Like a faithful dog.

She kept me busy all day,
Such a demanding guest.

Almost loud enough,
To drown out
My own mind, but
Alas, the thoughts of my unorganised brain
Never can be silenced, can they?

The wind still hasn't left,

I've spent hours,

Listening to her mindless pattering,

Her shrieking laughter,

The clicking of her shoes.

I've spent hours, waiting

For her to leave.

But,

I fear, I might be getting used to her,

Her noise,

Her voice,

Her presence,

For she fills the void you leave me with.

(All of it)

I've never told you,

'least not to your face,

But I never knew,

Till you told her,

That we were over.

I remember,

When you told me,

It wasn't okay,

While I sobbed to you on the phone.

And I remember joking,

About you not caring,

If I woke tomorrow as soul.

When I told my friends,

Their eyes widened,

And dear old me couldn't tell what was wrong.

Sometimes I bring up

My friends knowing more

About how ended

Than you'd care to remember

And I don't know if you're offended,

But I notice,

The face that you make,

And I hope that one day, you'll correct my mistake.

I think you know,

The day you told me you barely know me,

There were tears in my eyes,

Because I thought you were listening,

I thought you tried,

To remember,

But hey,

I guess I'm still forgotten and brushed aside.

(Is it that simple?)

I've had friends and foes,
Alike,
Some, which I have chosen.
Some, which chose me.

Some, I made,
With my own two hands,
Some, I watched grow.
And some, unexpected,
Found me.

But
There you are,
With your fly-away hair.

And there you are,
With your wandering hand,

Your unstoppable mind,

Inescapable charm,

Your hurtful, sweet eyes,

Your cold brutal heart,

And I wonder,

Just how,

Did I ever call you my friend,

And just what

would it take,

For me to do it

Again.

(To force a heart to stop hoping)

They say,
Healing takes time,
But how much
Longer
Do I need to stop
Waiting for your love,
To come back for me.

Because I'm
Still standing,
Perfectly stiff,
Trying so hard to
Breathe,
But
There's dust

Settled in my lungs,

Handprints

On my waist,

My glass eyes,

Are shattered,

And I,

Smiling.

(Ideally, you wouldn't)

I live in a world,

Where the sun shines

And the flowers don't wait for spring.

They smile when you

Stop to talk to them,

The hills are kind,

The trees shelter you.

The creatures bring you comfort.

I live in a world that radiates

So

Much

Warmth that you almost don't notice

The boiling lake of blood.

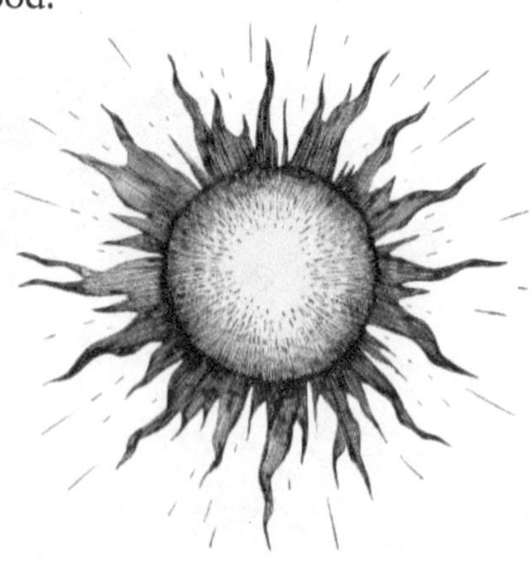

(Even in death, there are flowers)

[or the one Esha and I wrote.]

You buried our love in a graveyard,

But flowers bloomed from the bones which remained

And as I made them into rings,

It reminded me of how we were,

Always untamed.

And like

Flowers

Grown from bones,

Standing tall above my head,

Swaying in the wind,

With our words

Left unsaid

Falling from our lips

And burning us to the ground.

Oh, all the longing

That rested in pleasant heartache,

Dissolves, with not a home around.

(Maybe: ii)

Sometimes I talk to my friends,
About you, us,
And I start to question
Things I've never bothered.

'Maybe's float around my mind,
Maybe it wasn't my fault,
Maybe you weren't that pretty—
I was just in love,

Maybe it wasn't love—
Maybe I just wanted your affection.

Maybe it wasn't even affection—
Just my need for attention to fulfil.

Maybe your lack of emotion,

Came from an instinct of protection

Maybe all my devotion,

Wasn't a waste,

Maybe you loved me too much,

That's why you ran away.

(and maybe lying to myself will take the pain away.)

(Perhaps death will finally bring peace)

If it all shall end
Tomorrow,
'least you've held me,
And in your arms
And your lies,
'least I've been loved.

And if tomorrow,
You shall end me,
'least I've made peace.

(For safekeeping)

There are certain things

That I'd never tell you.

Like the way I felt each brush of your hand

Or every word you said,

I'd memorised it all

Each fingerprint, every glimpse

All those things you made me feel,

Everything I'd loved,

Everything I'd hated.

For somethings are better

Remained in my memories.

(Your mother once smiled at someone's coffee eyes)

If the years go back,
And my children go look through,
The pages of my life,
Tell them the story
Of my first wedding.

Tell them of the dim-lit room,
Of the faint white lamp.
Tell them the way we felt,
Intoxicated, on nothing at all.

Let them relish in their young mother's frivolous joy,
The temporary, unabashed euphoria,
Let them remember,
The strawberry lip balm,
They never tasted.

Let them imprint our smiling faces,
Deep as far as their mind goes.

For when I am at last, gone,
Let this be how our love lives on.

The aftermath

(Ah, I've found the sun)

I sit by the window,
And gaze
out, I look,
At the moon as she glistens.

Stars light up,
The black of my pen,
A million galaxies spread across,
A thousand worlds,
Peer into mine,
I reach for you
Across a billion skies,
Fading dark.

A hand finds my finger
Tips my palm to its side,
For a minute,

My delusional mind starts to wonder if it's you,

But soon an unmistakable light,

Binds itself to my soul

And as the warmth sets in,

There realisation sits.

(Round 2?)

Darling you'd always stood tall,

Even in those halls,

Where the only thing I wanted—

Was to dissolve

But I'd remember catching you,

Stall, in the mirror's reflection

And your hands fall again to your sides,

And your smile had permanently etched its way to my mind

And oh—my dear,

This wasn't supposed to happen

I wasn't supposed to give away again,

My all wasn't supposed to stray again,

And we were supposed to stay just friends.

But now my breath catches in my throat,

And oh I know—

I know how this story goes.

(New beginnings, I've learnt a lot)

I'd give everything

To see your eyes

Search for mine

Among clouded skies

As the wind beats the nights,

And oh, do you remember that day

The promise I made?

Your friend's ring,

The tears in mine's eyes

And darling, maybe not forever,

But for all my might,

I'd give it all to see us dancing that night.

(There's going to be a million forevers)

Slowly, gently, just fall
—with me, instead of for me
Just jump off the cliff together
We'll never look back,
Maybe
We might just make it out alive
—and if we do,
Then, slowly, gently, take my heart.
Take my words,
And with them, take my soul.
Darling, I'll try to hold yours
Forget forever—fall with me.
Fall with me right now.

(But, alas, I'm still learning.)

Here I am again,

Stood,

In a cold dark room.

I've been here before,

But

I think you know that too.

Last time,

It felt unfamiliar,

Somewhere I didn't think

I'd be anymore.

But this time,

I think I'd like to linger,

A bit more,

Maybe I'll

hang up my pictures,

decorate it with my scriptures

stuck to the wall,

And this time,

That won't be all.

For this time,

When I'll fall, I'll fall to embraces

Where I won't feel unsure.

And even unsaid words, will be enough.

(A carefully drawn map)

And that's how it'd start,
With simple hand holding
And promises of forever,
With "however many you'd like"
And blue ball-pen hearts
Hands intertwined through dinner
And glances from across rooms.

And this is how it'll end
With phone calls
And long-winded texts
Just three words
And all my friends' concerns.

(Things change, sometimes I stay the same)

The coming of the summer
Has brought me
Changes, far more than I can
Begin to describe.

The shifts, though,
I can still feel,
And so,
The current of the wind.

My flowers dry out,
Pretty pink, wilting leaves.

And changes, the water
Its taste.
That was, in the winter,
Sweet,
Leaves now salt,
At its feet.

But though the summer
Brought me tears,

Those tears, I bottle
To save,
Maybe, one day,
I may,
Sprinkle them gently,
On the daisies,
And help them make space,
For the arrival,
Of a new day.

(Am I still the sun?)

Now I'm close to tears,

Sat in my parents' car

But they won't come out,

No, not yet

For I have a question to ask you

Before I let my eyes get wet.

So, tell me, darling,

Are you telling me a story,

Or are these just your thoughts?

Do you still feel their words,

Or are they just like stars, long lost?

For I've told you

Every how, when, and why

And now it is your turn to answer,

And my turn to pry.

("Your existence is a menace sometimes.")

I'd love you just as much,
If you were simply a bug on my wall.

Even if you were insignificant to everybody else,
Closest to my heart you'd lie.

Even if there'd be a thousand others screaming,
You'd be the first voice I'd hear.

And though you'd misinterpret what I said,
For you, I'd forever keep repeating.

And though my heart would
Forever remain fleeting,
There'd be two who'd keep it.

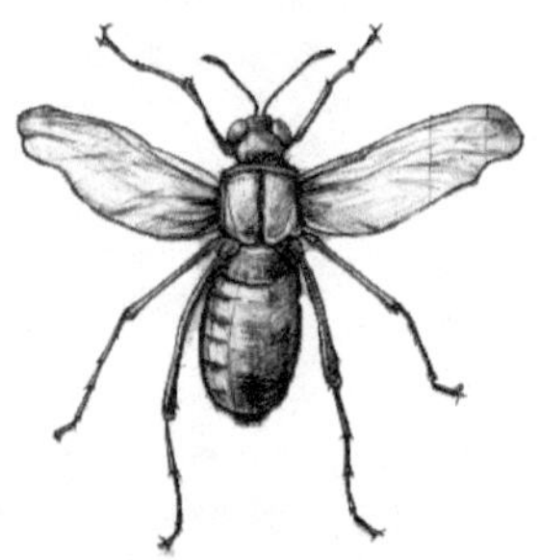

(201)

I used to beg, for consistency,
For permanence.

Used to think I would
spend my life
In a singular space,
Unmoving.

But now, I look back,
—it's been a year, maybe 2?
And some 3 months—

I examine my life,
And how it has changed.

All I thought consistent
Has long gone.

I bade farewell with a smile,
For the time has come and we move on
And better things find us.

And now I think
I might stay here a while,
As I unpack my things.

Reminders of discarded hobbies,
Books I'll never forget and the ones
I can't remember owing,
Pink balloons from my 13th,

They hang up my curtains,
As we laugh,
And the light's imperfect,
My walls are pink.

There's a lump in my throat,
As I pile up my writing,
And just maybe,
It is home this might just be.

Alina Vitto

(Healing at last)

In the earliest hours
of the morning,
or the latest of the night,
I sit awake,
This time not
because of the gaze
of a stranger,
or a love unreturned,
But simply because
Of the solitude
That I've found in my dark.
The quiet comfort of words
—some mine, some borrowed—
And the whisper of early morning light,
The slow pulse of heart
No more, longing or aching
But resting
Maybe not yet asleep,
But finally at peace.

(A different us)

I can still smell you on my skin,

And my friends aren't particularly fond of it,

When they smell you on my fingertips.

But I love you so, unconditionally,

In the purest way love can be

That I can't bring myself to care

If it is hubris to believe,

I pity the ones who shall never feel the same as we.

(Even I tell lies)

I plant seeds of

big white flowers

in my every word,

And hope that you never find them,

For if you did, you'd immediately recognise them.

You wouldn't question me,

Neither of you ever did—

But there would be this look

That I've memorised

Because it's the same as hers

It would be a question in your eyes,

But a smile on your face

And there's something you'd like to say,

But alas, you'd be too late.

(Catharsis?)

I remember,

Myself,

Sat on the floor,

Knees to my chest,

Back against the door,

I'd brace myself

Wait for the last tear

To fall

Right from my eyes,

Past rose coloured cheeks,

Down my neck,

Making my heart its home.

The same heart,

That thundered

And roared, and wailed

The one that felt

Oh, so much, and didn't

Deserve to be thrown and failed.

But the same heart
Now loved, and lost, and
Got back up again.

And it sits,
On the same floor,
Tucked away under
Someone's chin,
With the music on
A bit too loud.

Or with a magazine
In hand,
Pink rug on the floor
And laughter, hidden
In sleepy eyes.

And—oh it smiles,
Like the winter's sun approaching,
The heartbreak of the summer
Long dusted.

And things changed,
And tears glistened
But they created lakes
And watered flowers,
And in their wake,
Left a trail of powder
Tracing right back

To their eyes
And their smiles.

That we've accepted,
Now, as ours.

(Maybe: iii)

Maybe it's the sunlight,
On a Sunday morning,
Or
Maybe it's 3 am,
On a Saturday, when I'm prancing
Around my friends.

But there's this
Feeling,
That seems to be nagging,
Knocking,
Lingering.

It builds,
Like, an outburst of melancholy,

Bubbles,
Like joy, fluttering,
Like the gentle brush of my hands,
Against yours and theirs.

It cracks,

Like our collective laughter.

And it's rough, like her words,
Soft, like her voice

And it reminds me,
Of a lost time,
Of a garden, I planted, in the winter,
Long dead by the doorway,

And as it glitters in my chest,
I think,
I'd like to keep it there.

(Maybe this is a good place to be.)

Afterword

I seem to have existed
For everyone,

I've gathered every bit of
Pain,
That you've felt,

I've carried my own,
Wordlessly,

I've written apologies,
I've listened to everyone,

I've been talked over and,
Brushed aside
Looked at weird,
And smiled through it.

And I won't stop,
I can't.

But when this exhausting existence,
Is finally over,
I hope you find me,
In prose,
In empty notebooks,
In yellowed pages.

I hope you see
Incomplete poems, and the warmest of words
And see my face.

(That would be an honour enough.)

Since we're pretending this is a book,

Acknowledgments?

I know exactly where to start with this, because as every writer does, I've practised and prepared for this moment like an aspiring actor prepares for their acceptance speech.

Let me, first, explain myself. I started writing this with 'Euphoria', at my grandparents' house (affectionately named Pathargarh), in the midst of the second wave of a pandemic we thought we'd defeated. At that point, I was truly unaware of whatever was to come. In the months, and then the year that followed, I've witnessed my trust be built to impossible extents, then completely shattered, and rebuilt from the pieces. Making the decision to still have these people in my life was arguably one of the easiest decisions I've had to make. It went without thinking, that I couldn't live without them. So, learning to do just that, while knowing that they were there, and would be there if I ever asked, wasn't easy in the slightest. And, while I do not claim to be completely healed, I think, slowly, but surely I'm getting there. The poems you've just read are an encapsulation of everything that helped me get here. These are truly pieces of my heart and soul, and I trust you to keep them safe.

Secondly, let me apologise. To the subject of my poems, I'm well aware of how called out you might be feeling. For that, I shall try to apologise, and pretend that the evil flicker of happiness I felt is, 'least for the moment, non-existent. And to anyone who has, like me, felt alone while being completely surrounded by people, I'm sorry. Know that you will be better, know that this will pass.

Thirdly and finally, let me thank everyone and everything who've brought me to where I am today.

When I wrote my first poem, it was for a stupid school thing. So, let's start there. Thank you to that one school thing that made me write 'euphoria' and in turn allowed me to fall in love with poetry. Thank you to 'hamilton' for kick-starting my poem-writing-frenzy and to Lin-Manuel Miranda for writing it. To Taylor Swift, for creating the soundtrack of my life and for connecting me to some of my favourite people. To every author I grew up reading.

Thank you to my parents,

My mother, for not really understanding, but listening regardless, for being my best friend, and for teaching me the great comfort that is expression.

My father, for being over-enthusiastic, for introducing me to the stage that later became my safe place, and for not letting me give up on the things I loved.

To the rest of my family,

I know when you read these, you'll wonder what (and let's be honest, who) they're about, and while I won't tell you that, I hope you'll enjoy them regardless.

To my bedroom, my only home and my favourite place. Thank you for containing me as I learned and failed, for being patient with me and for being the birthplace of all of my poetry.

At the time of writing a vast amount of my poems, I'd felt completely isolated, bar one person. I was on my own for two years. I had no friends I could reach. And no friends to miss. And when that one person wasn't there, I lost sense.

A lot has changed since then. I am at last making peace with my own, and I've discovered once more, just how much comfort and how much understanding I could give my own self.

And for that, thank you to my friends, the most important people in my life, who all ultimately became my muses.

Dhruv, Aleya and Khushi, for never letting me be upset, and for being supportive of my writing, without ever reading it. I wouldn't have made it through the last half without you.

To Aleya, and for teaching me to hate. I'm hoping you'll read this cover to cover. But that might be asking too much. For what it's worth, I'll always love you.

(PS: to Khushi, the font size is 13, thank you for giving Chamak Challow its identity, and just generally being so invested in all of my journals.)

And again, to Dhruv, for always questioning me; I need that more than I'd like to admit, for telling me to stop, I need that too.

Eshanya, for talking me through the worst of it and for always understanding. I don't know how I found you, but I'm going to keep you for as long as possible. I love you so much, jaan.

Inshra di, for so many things I won't mention, for being the one person I could say anything to, for being my most trusted, and for always supporting me, no matter which poorly thought-out endeavour I went on.

Anushka, my favourite person, for re-reading everything I ever wrote to you 5 million times. You can keep it with you forever now. I love you.

To Amaira, thank you for always being there, even when nobody else was, thank you for not letting me be alone again. Thank you for always understanding. I hope this makes it way on your bookshelf, I hope this can be one of your favorite books. I love you.

And most importantly, to Nehal, my best friend, first reader and the reason I began writing in the first place. There's still so much left of everything I want to say to you, but I think I've told you enough. I hope one day, our skin will be permanently marked with remainders of what we had and what we have. Thank you for being my only support system for so long, for holding my hand and heart till I found my way, and at last, for always staying. Pack me in your suitcases and make me a stowaway, will you?

About Alina

Alina is an enigmatic voice that dances between the realms of words and emotions, capturing the experience of young love and it's consequent heartbreak in her debut poetry collection. Born with a heart attuned to the subtle symphonies of life, Alina's journey as a poet began amidst the tranquil landscapes of her childhood, where she found solace in the verses of timeless poets and the whispers of nature.

Her first book, titled "Things Change, sometimes I stay the same" delves into the labyrinth of the ever-fleeting human emotions, exploring the delicate threads that connect joy, sorrow, love, and longing.

Frob
Friends of books
Download app at
www.frob.social

Social
App for
Readers

Explore Books
on wide subjects

Join/Create
Book Clubs

See
Booktalk
Videos

Interact with
noted Authors and
like-minded readers

INKFEATHERS PUBLISHING

www.inkfeathers.com

We love creating beautiful books for you!

Come be a part of our ever-growing community of authors. Grow, write, and publish with us!

Scan here to explore books, authors and more

Connect with us on socials. We'd love to hear from you!

    Inkfeathers Publishing